The High Road to Taos

The High Road to Taos

MARTIN EDMUNDS

University of Illinois Press   URBANA AND CHICAGO

Some of these poems have appeared in the following publications, several of them in slightly different form: *Agni, Arvon International Poetry Competition Anthology* for 1987, *Boulevard, Grand Street, The Nation, New Yorker, Padan aram, Paris Review, Partisan Review, Pinchpenny, Southwest Review,* and *Under 35: The New Generation of American Poets* (Anchor/Doubleday 1989).

This book is printed on acid-free paper.

Library of Congress Cataloging-in-Publication Data
Edmunds, Martin, 1955-
    The high road to Taos : poems / by Martin Edmunds.
        p.   cm. — (National poetry series)
    ISBN 0-252-06404-6 (paper)   BT 10.95/9.42-1/95
    I. Title. II. Series.
PS3555.D482H5 1994
811'.54—dc20   93-44944
                                                                           CIP

The National Poetry Series

The National Poetry Series was established in 1978 to publish five collections of poetry annually through five participating publishers. The manuscripts are selected by five poets of national reputation. Publication is funded by the Copernicus Society of America, James A. Michener, Edward J. Piszek, the Lannan Foundation, and the Andrew W. Mellon Foundation.

1993 Competition Winners

Rafael Campo, *The Other Man Was Me: A Voyage to the New World*
    Selected by Gloria Vando, published by Arte Publico Press.

Martin Edmunds, *The High Road to Taos*
    Selected by Donald Hall, published by the University of Illinois Press.

Karen Swenson, *The Landlady in Bankok and Other Poems*
    Selected by Maxine Kumin, published by Copper Canyon Press.

Rachel Wetzsteon, *The Other Stars*
    Selected by John Hollander, published by Viking Penguin.

Kevin Young, *Most Way Home*
    Selected by Lucille Clifton, published by William Morrow and Co.

For Carol Moldaw

Contents

I

The High Road to Taos

I. Taos

> Morning comes to life
> with the grating of shovel and pick.
> Wind shrills like a fife
> in the reeds. Against the heraldic
>
> escutcheon of sunrise
> stands the red bull, black
> as the shadow of the morada
> that never dries.
>
> Sharp stones, wind, thorns, and wild
> water staring in puddles.
> The Campo Santo huddles
> its shoulders against the cold.
>
> The Campo Santo sits
> jostled among small hills.
> Its tenants are done with dawn's
> pink slips and unpaid bills.

They sleep. The starved eye feeds
on winter deaths, the red
dirt piled high above
each temporary bed.

Big-bellied, each fresh grave's
a woman giving birth.
When the meek inherit the earth,
this is the acre they get.

They have been carried across
the bridge that skims the river.
Their bodies were bathed in the front room,
their hearts in the Guadalquivir.

They have been carried across
the river and the ditch.
Their headstones line up like the chairbacks
of boys in the orphanage

of the Government Indian School.
In every scraggly row,
one tilts at a perilous angle.
Wet whips dangle

from the weeping willow.
They have entered the iron vault
of earth. Under a turned-up
barrow, they swallow her salt—

what in our mouths, too, will be,
with the flinty sparks of stars,
the taste of eternity
when the cortege of cars,

in a cloud of dust, withdraws,
and all is barrenness.
The wind its passage raised
is shaking in the haws.

II. A Hill Village.
    One of Los Hermanos de Sangre, the Brothers of Blood, Speaks.

Filling the grooves of his name,
a late spring snow
blots out the black pain
of Innocencio

from his marble stone,
swallowing all sound
where he lies within
the barbwired holy ground.

Good Friday. Viernes Santo.
The death of every bell.
Mirrors, being punished,
turn and face the wall.

'Mano! Remember Christmas?
Season of bells and meat!
And the basins ringing last night
for the washing of the feet.

The church doors left wide open
to the mild night air.
And the smiling dog who trotted
in to say her prayer.

Spiritus Sanctus
whispered the bells at Mass.
The snow, immaculate,
falls into the razor grass

where my brothers leave
pink stains beneath bare feet.
Confess! Confess! Confess!
hisses the freezing sleet.

The feminine wail of the flute
weeping over the scales.
The bass drum in my temples
that drives home the nails.

Snowflakes soft as ash
stirred by the wind around
the slow arc of the lash
float upward and descend

burning, now, to pour
into the sacred sign,
the three cuts near my spine
slit by the Picador.

He makes veronicas
with the gonfalon.
The white bull of the wind
grazes his bloodied hand.

The fraying nerves of the fife.
Cessation of every sound
for the Procession of Blood
in which the bells are drowned.

III.   The Morada. La Muerte.

Death stands straight in her cart.
Her nose is in the air,
although she has no nose.
She aims the poisoned dart
of her breath at us.
Her arrow-hand is swift.
Her knuckles, scabbed with bark,
will not relax their grip
until the arrow-tip
lies quivering in its mark.

Pray for a good death,
but what death is good?
Her eyes outstare our eyes.
Her kisses are wormwood.
We breathe her waxen breath.
Death's sunken bust endures
while we, who were so beau,
so cool, so free of care,
and young, my friend, qué no?—
approach her on all fours.

IV.   El Santuario de Chimayó.

Guillermo tells everyone
Guillermo sold the field
because the earth, no virgin,
got stinting in her yield.

And the only *huero*
he can tolerate
is the barley straw
beneath his horse's feet.

But Guillermo doesn't own a
horse so far this year.
"¡Qué lástima!" he sighs
into his Corona.

"The only *huero* I like
is the blond head on my beer."
"¡Cerveza!" he cries. *"¡Cerveza!"*
A cry cried from the heart.

A fair-haired man
sucks down his Coors,
afraid the holy service
is about to start.

The line for the taco stands
blends into the line for church
and the line for the PortaSans.
Pigeons coo from their perch.

Inside, perpetual dusk
becoming the dark night.
Once your eyes adjust,
everything's red or white.

A sword glints white. The Lord's
discarded robe is red.
A red baldric for the carpenter
who nails him to the boards.

Hanging from a tack,
spine arched against the splintery
timber, thick neck thrust
hard against the cross,

eyes open but rolled back,
a terrible Christ.
His upper, unforgiving
teeth look very sharp.

A bloodless Reconquest!
From the height of a cloudy alp,
San Rafael angles his coup stick
toward a dripping scalp.

To the right, above,
fluttering on a disc,
wings of a white dove,
a sprig of tamarisk.

Filing past the altar's
gaily painted rail,
teens in tanks and halters
hide out from the hail.

One couple stands apart.
He rubs her arms, bare.
Her hand strokes his cheek
and rests lightly there.

They have taken a vow of silence
until the *matraca* strikes three.
They have no need for words.
Anyone can see.

9

Watching how their hearts
smoke in a green cage,
I smell bees and blood.
I see my wife at that age.

I'd confess my sins,
I'd confess my lies,
just to be able to look
like that into her eyes.

We pass into the room
favored by the tours—
the testimonials
of miraculous cures.

Assorted canes and crutches
hang from the ceiling beams.
Two saints in fly-screened hutches
hear confessions and dream.

Sharp click of billiard balls
comes from the monks at their beads.
A forest of walking sticks
is climbing up the walls.

There's Santiago Matamoros
hung with purple hearts and keys,
dogtags, scapulars,
licenses, rosaries.

Saint "Death-to-the-Moors!" James
and his whole platoon
might be reactivated.
(There's an election soon.)

Next to three plaster San
Franciscos de Asís,
Mary cradles her son
across her ancient knees.

On the wall behind her,
(wearing their hats in church!)
snaps of two policemen
and one of their murderer.

Rosewater's splashed on her hands.
The window, opened a crack,
lets in a gust of onions
from the taco stands.

There's a picture of Guadalupe
—a mosaic, I mean—
made with cherry, menthol, and lemon
cough drops and black beans.

There's El Santo Niño
in a cockle hat; a shell,
scalloped, briny, gilded,
on his rich lapel.

Expectant mothers whisper
in the pink shell of his ear;
missing children leave him
their old shoes to wear.

Piercing the inner dark,
a burning fishhook trolls
its barbed question mark
where a bare bulb glares down

over women crying in Spanish,
over a white dish,
over San Rafael
with his string of gutted fish.

Hot wax fumes and drips
onto a tile beside
a china Magdalena,
real lipstick on her lips.

There's a xeroxed photo,
taken by his wife,
of a man who disappeared
in 1988,

last seen in Española
by the Duke City gate.
It's stapled to a brief
description of his clothes—

brown pants, brown shirt, brown shoes,
and his red tattoos—
JESÚS on his left arm,
on his right, a rose.

There's a photo of La Muerte
in her chariot,
beside a saint with raised
finger to his lips—

Juan Nepomuceno,
patron of confessors?
—or Judas Iscariot?
Hanging from a rafter,

a frayed slingshot? A truss?
King David, reminding
the way we are living
will be the death of us.

A sign for *El Pozito*
points to a low door.
You bow your head to enter.
There's a dirt hole in the floor.

Hung on the mud wall,
a bloody Sacred Heart
proclaims in needlepoint
"Jesús es Amor!"

Like Lourdes, only more humble.
Not holy water, but holy dirt.
Untidy, lovely jumble
in four rooms, like the heart.

As the vigil proceeds
through the days of Holy Week,
more pilgrims eat in the courtyards;
some fast; some are just broke;

one hugs a five-foot cross
and a two-foot coke;
one nods off to the candles
whose prayers go up in smoke;

clutching a plastic bag
full of healing dirt,
a boy, shouting "Fag!"
throws stones at a man in a skirt;

old rivalries are decided
with jagged bottle or blade,
the river's drunken bragging
not to be gainsaid.

The Santa Cruz River
with its bank of blackened grass
holds in its swirling current
the woodgrain of the cross.

Snow falls. The river grumbles
through these poor acres, farmed
with a prayer and a blade,
where even the olive is armed

and rank as the rose with thorns.
It's either drought or flood,
the road washed out for good.
Spring's when the mother ditch burns,

when a bent back sustains
every two-crow field,
and the Sangre de Cristo Mountains
redden under the rains.

Riding the wind overhead,
little bloody whips
of silk trouble the eye.
They fall at our feet. The red

catkins hemorrhage
into river water, black
as the road that leads to this place
on the soul's pilgrimage:

highway of wooden crosses,
highway of Mexican bars,
highway of ditch bosses,
highway of knife-wounds and stars.

II

Fever

for Clara Edmunds

Nana whispers her prayers
to the book of sunlight open in her lap.
I squeeze my eyes hard.
Rain falls from clouds blowing in the playing marble
I clench under my pillow.

Time drips into the basin while I suck
an icicle's mercury tip, time probes
behind the black forehead throbbing on the map
of Africa tacked to my dresser, erasing the names
with swabs of Egyptian cotton dipped in alcohol.
The curtains are drawn as the book is shut.

Knives, forks, spoons being stacked,
a wet dishtowel snapped
clean as a rifle shot,
everything straightened up,
the broom's thump put back.

Someone drapes a cloth
over the lampshade. The room
is red, then grey, then grainy black
walls lean in to check on me,
breathing, and stroking my back.

My mother's face, a spray of lilac
shaken over me.

A C-train goes by.
Starting with Alpha Centauri, the stars
rattle in cobalt bottles on the shelf.

Like A Green Branch

The power blown, a candle
watched over us unsleeping.
Lying beside you, I heard
dark eaves dripping, dripping.

Wind shook
the wet night;
our roof lay open
to stormcloud and starlight.

Torn raw by each new gust,
drained white on the damp sheet,
your moans came slow, then fast.

I saw how the red rain
was smeared against the screen.
I could not reach your pain.

It still comes down, the rain
comes down. I wake up in the night.
My hands ache. They have kept
the feel of a green branch stripped
living from the bough
no match nor torch can light.

Stone,

teach me
to be like you, to take
a beating and keep
my mouth shut,
to carry the sun
in my stomach
deep into the night.

Going Out to Look
at the Year's First Blossoms

The tall, black, Nubian nanny,
chest-high, yellow-eyed,
pupils squinched down
tight as a vise,
regards me slyly.
Nuzzles my pockets,
ducking and backing.
Disgusted with nothing,
holds my gaze and
pisses into the spraddled ditch.

I leave her
fenced in the field,
breathing that steam.

A half hour later,
the first small blossoms,
white, still wet, delicate,
barely cling to their branch
in a breeze.

Returning, wading
last year's dried
seedpods on the ditchbank,
cresting the ridge, sharp
goatheads
burr my passage
from feet to knees.

What malice! What venom! What envy!
In the eyes of the goat!
In the teeth of the weeds!

One for the Road

A dusk so dark woodsmoke
is a hung net unkinking
until the sky opens
a scar of lightning,
forked road down which
a white-faced convict
looks back but comes stumbling.

Claws scrape at the cracked flags
lining the drive.
Red eyes seen through
the steam of its breathing,
sniffing me out.

Let it be.
Let what is leashed
and beaten in me
come and go begging
through the night, lifting

house after house,
city by city,
a torn silence, the bloody
pads of its paws.

At the eye of the storm,
unbearable calm.

Far down the evening,
a dog barks.

Just like that, a man
opens his throat to the moon.

Cabin Site
Christmas Island, N.S.

1.

Where three eagles cross in the sky
a dark shuttle flies
through the long afternoons.

Where three eagles cross in the sky
bury a bone
in the dark.

Where three eagles cross in the sky
a tooth
grinds on stone.

2.

The thudding Atlantic
under rain; spine
of hills through fog.

Ashes from the fire provide
the leavening for bread.
By sputtering candles
the small bodies
of the animals you've killed
do a quick dance
in the black pot, reduce
to a thick, grey stew.

Nights when the gloom lifts,
the cloud that hangs in the sky
pours its black milk on the land.
You call your first-born 'Moon.'

His teeth dig in.
You live off the pain
that lives off you, knowing
from generation
to generation, this
is what survives.

3.

Eyes
in the evening fire;
and today, pinned cruciform
on the sky an eagle:
two plies of darkness,
red-jeweled talons, blood on the wing.

Piri, you lean closer
to the squalling of the crows:

an eye that is a mouth,
a heart all hunger.

Monday

Bare bulb on a frayed cord, bad
connection. A loose tooth. Vinegar. Vinegar!

Appalachia

A woman watching
her daughter watching
rain dripping from twine.

The only iron they'll get
out of these hills
is the red stain fading
from a rag on the line.

November

The sun, bedded in mud,
hugging charred straw.

Through the chill wet,
a red-winged blackbird's orange epaulette.

That gashed coal catches.
The tinder glints.

Along the fens
reflecting Boston in a smoky lens,

dead reeds and glass sappers
through which the sucked blood comes.

The last wasp hums
in a bucket.

Bleached weeds sour
between a frost and a thaw.

I see, green-cheeked, needy,
how you'll come back to me.

December Frost

A raw, red haze gnaws
at the tops of the alders.

The sparse grass blades hiss
like steel on whetstones in your Necropolis.

My throat holds the crow's own
swallowed caw.

You're gone,
Father.

Nothing I say can make
the chill and dripping distances withdraw.

Letter to Jeffrey Gustavson

Today is one of those grey days sadder than a day of rain.
It has the eyes of a hurt woman who won't voice her complaint
or even face me. Nothing issues from her wound; only my own
presence taints the air. I tongue the sour iron tang of the wind's
scythe and taste the blade of yesterday's sunlight in salt hay
tangled on her nape, the iodine residues of nightsweats, so that
an oak leaf rusts, less red than a rose, in her unbraided hair.

The same grey sky welds everything I can see. It laps roof-
tiles and mortars the bricks on seven tipsy chimneys, it takes
a plaster cast of the twin, green-needled leaders of the cedar
tree, it dusts and lifts the whorled thumbprint of a firethorn
unleafed as yet, and the poplar which one more week will sheet
like the midmast of a clipper, a mile high, her stays and sails
spiced with dianthus pinks and shaking out mint in the luff,
but today, still bare, the poplar stand's a fossil of Christ's bony
fingers, his right hand raised to heaven, saying: "basta, Abba,
enough."

The reddish, beefy cast of brick dust adds body to the chalked
horizon line which creeps closer through the mist—everything

hedges inward, they all stare at me. Spring that delayed the last
two weeks because I was not ready to give up the after-winter wet
blacks and tans of tree bark is getting tired of me. Tell them
I do not want another hour, another fifteen degrees of daylight
to see what I'm eating by. The sunset was supper enough for me
through Lent, the turf itself, a mauve weave at my feet, gave
the illusion of pilgrimage to a sedentary life, it clothed me
in the scratchy sackcloths of burlap stripped from the magnolia's
roots, this window handed me a slate on which to sketch, or scratch,
my own violent likeness; and when the sun, the healer, completed
his grand rounds, he left piled on the horizon the pastel scrubs
from whole med schools of interns on rotations, faded from
one hundred and fifteen washings so far this year.

But each new sun that rises on my having finished nothing
rubs salt in a green wound; the moon sifts alum into my open eyes
from her dented tin measuring cup. That's why I pray only to work
in the aftermath of a bad winter through which I sat on my hands
to warm them, that's why I dig down with this pen and won't look up.

III

The Highlands 1966

for Sharon Edmunds

A boy is driving nails into the dirt.
A woman hangs her washing on the line.
A girl eats boiled peas from a single tine.

She crouches under her desk: Red Alert.
The sergeant whips his conscripts into line.
Clouds gather. The rain that comes is white and fine.

A woman takes her wash down from the line.
A boy is driving nails into the dirt.
A girl braids beads of rain on fraying twine.

Saigon. Friday. A little R&R.
The sergeant meets some women in a bar.
His daughter pastes a heart on a valentine.

The air is sharp and sour, the taste of time.
Leaf buds such raw reds looking makes him hurt.
A boy is driving nails into the dirt.

A boy is driving nails into the dirt.
Some scabs are picked for employment at this time.
Lawns whiten under a snow of bone and lime.

The sergeant takes two beauties in the spine.
The woman scorches her hand ironing a shirt.
She sobs into the pillow, "This does not hurt."

A hand explores the crotch of the apple tree.
Grasps in the rainy hole what he cannot see:
a fistful of steel eels, cold and—look now, shiny.

It is the sixth joyful mystery of the nails.
Who hid them in the tree in a paper sack?
And is whoever left them coming back?

Five candles on a cake. The woman turns forty.
The in-laws smile across the buffet line.
She toasts the chair opposite hers. The chair stays empty.

A bag is nailed inside a wooden box.
A boy's hand closes on a paper sack.
The dolly wheels leave streaks on the drying tarmac.

A boy is driving nails into the dirt.
A girl sticks out her tongue and closes her eyes.
A boy mustn't harm the beetles, the emerald flies.

A boy admires a bronzen beetle so tight it dies.
If they weren't so fast, he'd like to admire some flies.
A boy is driving nails into the dirt.

A flag is draped across a wooden box.
Harsh is the note the bugler's tongue attacks.
A gunshot rips sky cleanly—not slurred nor curt.

The cut earth cannot hold the opened hurt.
Mossed headstones cannot swallow the salute.
A boy is driving nails into the dirt.

Wet stains green the knees of a boy's new suit.
Harsh and sweet, the mowed hillside's report.
A boy's hand closes on a paper sack's

torn mouth. The flag is taken from the wooden box.
The air is turning blue from the breath of guns.
A boy's neck tickles where the holy water runs.

The clipped grass matches the crewcuts, dabbed with wax.
Peace is whispered as the missals shut.
The caps go on. White gloves hide hard handshakes.

"You do your sergeant proud, young soldier, but
that keen noise is a rifle, not a gun.
And never say 'Repeat.' Say 'Say again.'"

The half-mast flag lies limp on its sweating pole.
Mud clods rain down on the wooden box.
A white cloth swabs where spit bleeds from a weep-hole.

The bugler beds his horn in velvet. Night
commences when the case shuts with two clicks.
A woman does the dishes, checks the locks.

Ten treads smooth and cool beneath her feet.
A claw hammer by the headboard of a bed.
A woman dries a sleeping boy's drenched head.

The boy presses against her flesh for warmth and weight.
The way she cannot sleep without a sheet.
The boy whimpers. The woman bends to kiss his cheek.

A moth is beating at the shaded light.
Some ache of pleasure sets them suffering.
It is the season's first bad muggy night.

The boy's eyelids flutter, rising toward her height.
As if his mother's face were the source of light.
A moth is lying in the lamp's strict ring.

Her arches ache on every creaking tread.
The door won't shut, swollen by the night's damp heat.
Her palms smooth Truro's dunes on the empty bed.

She shivers. A glass sweats in the frosted light.
The woman cannot sleep. The tea's cold in her cup.
The faces in the wainscot won't come right.

The curtain's open. The night wind shakes out
lamplight on the lawn like a tablecloth.
Her hand weighs his lighter. Blue water. The leaping trout.

The flint strikes fire but the singed wick is dry.
The lamp clicks off. The walls hold their breath.
Her hand finds the hollow where he used to lie.

The sound of tearing grass. It's two a.m.
Next door, a spotlight makes its hourly sweep.
The neighbor was a grunt, just back from 'Nam.

Soft thump of clods tossed on a wire screen.
The woman worships in the church of night.
A saw is gnawing at the yard's last green.

The night is panting in the flower beds.
A steel blade grates on gravel. Stones click as he digs.
Sheets cling like seaweed to her naked legs.

The woman touches the wet glass to her lips.
False summer, with its real thirst and heat!
The sour sea's rising through the fresh-washed sheets.

Steam is seeping through the pillowcase.
The woman hugs her breasts. Salt scalds her face.
She rocks her body while the hot night weeps.

The woman cannot point to where it hurts.
Dawn reddens the edges of the blind. She sleeps.
A boy is driving nails into the dirt.

A woman stirs a stew of blue moons with a stick.
Cuffs and collars bob in the tub of suds.
A boy strikes sparks hammering caps on a chunk of brick.

A girl studies the colors on each stamp she licks.
A woman mails each brother one white shirt.
A boy is driving nails into the dirt.

A girl closes her eyes, sticks out her tongue.
Her nape beneath the veil feels the lace of eyes.
Monsignor wheezes. *Adoro te* is sung.

A girl poses by the Virgin all in white.
St. Joseph kneeling is the girl's same height!
A boy is driving nails into the dirt.

A woman curses, focusing the light.
The sun has scarlatina. A blood blister lids its eye.
White bisons wester, silent, through the sky.

A woman takes her wash down from the line.
A boy is driving nails into the dirt.
A girl is waiting for a certain sign.

A boy kneels, then sits on the tails of his father's shirt.
It rains. The apple ripens, but nothing happens.
A boy is driving nails into the dirt.

Albatross

Ungainly grounded, how do you bear it, two
too-little legs upholding you? Graceful, when
air-borne—a feather-cinctured lightness—
you of the delicate spirit, rise up!

Lancaster Street

1.

In June, when the star jasmine
brushes the world with its soft pollen
and even what's not truly beautiful
lifts its green head in the wind and sings,

we touched—not wittingly, and yet
not against our wills. If

it was love, it was
just the beginning, my senses still
upset by the warm season:

each sweet thing
tasting like the other thing.

2.

All that first evening, the star-clouds
thickened as the sky dimmed. The night that came
was curved and cool and double-dark;

so the rain went on, building
its green arcade
under a whitecapped wave of lilacs
breaking on the garden wall.

We sat up
in the top of the house,
the French doors
propped open to admit
what breeze there was,
and listened

to each raindrop's tap
on the tar-paper, the new gutter
gurgling, giving up
its oiled sheen to the sheer

run-off. The roof beams
creaked in a single swelling.

After a rain like that, what door would close?

3.

Oh, there were signs all right:
handle floating northward
out of reach, the dipper
tipped in darkness its bowl
of nothing on the night.

October came, wading
the meadow, saying
in the noon-lit, knee-high, raspy
whisper of turkey grass:

all this lightness
passes.

At dusk the dullest aspen spoke
nothing I could understand,

but, when I turned my back,
the river murmured: *leave*

what you love;
love leaving instead.

4.

The answer was easy.
We approached the garden,
pruned back the roses and the lilacs,
exposing the white grid of a trellis
against a bare, white wall.

The work could have been done
in a week-end, but we started late
and gave up early Sunday night
under amber window light, in rain.

We retreated to the high room,
closed the French doors against the cold,
then sat for hours and smoked. I knew
that you were beautiful, and thought:

she will go away.

Later, I spoke:
"In the morning
there will be words

that come together like separate
panes of glass over which
one tint of light
bleeds and passes."

Half lit, half
in shadow, abstracted,
as if reading the absent stars,
you said:

"Expect to find
no special thread of sorrow."

5.

It is almost June again. Day comes,
already dulled by the usual sadness
when the pre-dawn din of gulls falls
silent, and I watch it begin.

But now, as I write you, I remember
how the sun burned clear through the summer;
how, before dawn, I'd wake
to watch the night go
trailing its thatched shadow;

each September noon
hummed with the bees that wove
their one thread of gold
through the garden's patterned colors;

not thinking at all
how that dusk the sun
would pale on the wall.

Farewell

Farewell, my love, goodbye.
Red wine, and oyster pie,
and all the good times too
are going with you.
Farewell, my love, adieu.

Because the way your wrist
moved when you let your hair
uncoil to hide us there
in the crowded street where we kissed,
farewell, my love, goodbye.

The tender green of spring,
so fresh, so pale, so new,
a green haze on everything
easily torn in two.
Farewell, my love, adieu.

Because when you lean in the door,
slipping the shoes from your feet,
not knowing—how would you know?—
the light's not the same as before.
Farewell, my love. Please go.

Because of how you tie
your hair, because your ear,
its whorl, connects the sweep
of jaw to dark-downed nape
all night while you sleep,
farewell, my love, goodbye.

Because your bare neck, bent
above these words, will lead
to moonlight lying like snow
on windowsill, on white
throat, on lid, on cheek,
on your lips wet with wine,
and the bed's dishevelment.
Farewell, my love, goodbye.
It would be better if you went.

Because what never was,
how could it come to be?
How can this heart be mine?
It was small, but grew
so large loving you
it won't fit back in me.
Farewell, my love, adieu.

The words that we have said,
the raw edge of the sky,
and the brown earth hurts me too
because of you.

Farewell, my love, goodbye.
Red wine, and oyster pie,
and all the good times too
are going with you.
Farewell, my love, adieu.

One Look at the Creation

for Carol Moldaw

1.

Already, the rain and cold
rotting a token leaf,

later, the glittering snow,
tomorrow the dark, a blustery sleep,

but today, alone, and nearer
to you than me, the rain

comes down forever. I bless it
and I let it go.

2.

Beyond the flash and fire, the golden
linden reaping its glorious self,
you are the wind I love, the only

other breath that I can be.

In Memoriam: Robert Fitzgerald

Listen how the river berates me: all one
glittering motion.

Egypt

for Alexander

A lapis sky. No moon. The evening stars,
Venus in the southwest,
reddish Mars,
Nut's hennaed nipples, the left one wet with milk.
I have sucked them. I shall never die!

Chromo

My head is open.
Green smoke of the morning has opened it.
Come climb inside it!

My heart is open.
Red smoke of the sun has opened it.
Come climb inside it!

My arms are open.
Blue smoke of the mountains has opened them.
Come climb inside them!

I Have Tried to Find You

for Lavinia Currier

I have tried and I have tried to find you.
I have sent my mind out towards you:
blank walls! bare rooms!
Everything empty and white, except
on a white pine table, in a drinking glass,
the white flame of a candle mantles its wings and burns.

I have sent my spirit out in search of you—
cold winds moaning alone over mountain peaks;
purple evening deepening to the note
of a blown conch, steeped in the sea
and blue as the *o* in soul.

I have sent my heart out to look for you
and it comes back daubed wet with red clay
from a riverbed, beginning to dry
and crack in the sun.

Now I send my love out on four winds,
and ask it to come towards you down the path
you are traveling, to be the first green thing your eye
lights on one morning, to find you and stay with you
and not come back to me.

I wish I were green rain in a grass field,
or green-gray rain
in an orchard of olives, or warm rain with a soft
green-gold wind in it, or white rain
falling softly through blossoms of apples,
or the wind, or wind-blown sunlight itself,
so I could hold you in my arms which are not my arms,
so you could rest in me
the way the Bradford pear, under its burden of petals,
clusters of still-wet stars,
leaned its new weight on the daylight in the park
an hour ago,
so my heels could spark a circle of white flames
about your feet,
so you could feel how the light loves you
as it wants to do.

Willows Coming Into Leaf

To have seen, to have held you
naked under your dress
in your green silk slippers, Spring!

Thirteen Years

for Carol Moldaw

A calla lily in a tulip skirt,
top lip thinner than a paper cut—
I knew by looking how that lip could hurt.
I wanted to take you into my arms, but
I saw it would be life.
Your calves were curved like the blade of a butter knife.
Your bottom lip brimmed, a raindrop on a vine.
Bitten, it took the blush of summer wine.

That night your body had a hundred lips
cool as new leaves curled against the rain,
each leaf thirsty for my fingertips
that held the calm eye of the hurricane
caught in their whorls and circling breasts, thighs, hips,
till touching made you want my mouth again.

It took me time to trust
that I was born for this,
for the hint of rose in the dusk
that gathers in your eyelids' mildest folds,
for the salt sea taste
of the tidemark where a string of kisses chased
the tanline across your shoulders and under each breast—
pale upturned poplar, leaf that I love best—
and the cinnamon dusting your belly, its thin line
arrowing downwards to a mossy place,
for your thighs whose blue veins trace
my private silk route to the lands of spice,
for the star chart marked in your palm that's pressed to mine.

Thirteen years, woman.
Now, when I drink you down,
you are water not wine.
Charmed water where my thirst
deepens as it nears its source.

Weathering

for Carol Moldaw

A hammer, a bagful of staples, five strands of wire
can't keep moonlight or the black stallion off the mare.
The wind is from the west. The wind is a green fire.
The willow shivers, naked under her hair.

Falling stars drift down in piles beneath the pear.
Remember last August, my desire
dying down like roses from toothed leaf to bud?

The drugged hive pulses. Sap drips. Dust is mud.
I want you.
This is the bees' season in the blood.

Passion Week
Monday After Palm Sunday

Last week I saw myself with green ivy sprouting from the cen-
tre of my forehead; before I could tend to one growth, a second
would appear, and then a third, by which time the first had begun
to wither. But none of them died, they just hung on dried out
and near dead.

If I held you in my arms now, Lent would end. The sharp,
black spikes on the wrought-iron railing of the deck next door
would relent and melt, twist down like candles exposed all day
to the summer sun, the ache of its curved blades, the chrome
harrow, the candles on the hearse at Tenebrae. Those deep purple
morning glories would unfurl the night sky in the heart of the day.
The moon and sun both would shine down from the night sky
and the day sky would leap beneath the sea, whose surface would
take on the radiance.

If I held you in my arms now I believe a star would dive
down the darkness of my throat and glow there, a live rose or
coal, twin to the star in your heart; and to talk we would need

only to see the light spill from all our pores. Then our flesh
would shine like gold grain in a sieve, rinsed and rinsed,
incorruptible.

But you right now are warm sunlight falling all along my arms;
and sometimes you are the welcome drops of awakening rain. How
could I not love you? How could a man not love the sun, the moon,
the stars, the curved paths of the planets arcing like raindrops down
glass, like shiny stretchmarks on the belly of the black-skinned
mother of all, night? How could a man not love the night
itself; the smells of night, of sweat, of sex, of wet earth and
dead leaves, the lily whose scent is heavy as drenched silk,
cool and profuse, its oil, wet silk rubbed between finger and
thumb? How could a man not love the smell of wet, blond straw
rotting and turning black in the rose beds? Of tide flats at new,
at neap, at full, their smell of spoiled eggs, of salt and salt-
pocked metal and spilled blood? How could a man not love the
flood tide, a raw wind lifting the smell of salt off the sea?
How not love the smell of fresh rain lifting in sheets of white
gauze cotton billowing across the dunes? When have I not loved,
at the new moon, your smell of blood and smoke? and at the full,
the sweet milk scent and your breasts pendulous, white as the milk
rising in stems of spring weeds, my head resting in the hollow
between your breasts marked with a dark star, like lying between
swales of new-mown grass? When have I not loved the smell of the
blown rose and the rose just opening? How could a man not love
the thin green sheaves of reeds beginning to spring up now from
tufty clumps in the salt marsh, the fens, and other low-lying
places, though his bare arms and hands sting still where they
have been razored by those canes? How not love the cream foam
left by the mower, and later, white salt caked on mud in the
sucky furrow, blood on the blade?

How could I not love, lifting the soft, mossy tendrils, brushing my lips on the resistless down, the freshwater smell still clinging to your nape, a thin stream spilling into bruised moss, clay, the green-blue hues of slate shading into the dust and taste of sucked stones? And the white, crescent, cool moons under your breasts that smell sometimes of hay, sometimes of pebbles taken from a river bed? Or the sun-warmed flesh of your belly, your ribs, thin crescent-leaved willows dipping to touch, blue and green, sky and leaf, the warm, burnished skin of the river, the smell of warmth itself on the first mild summer night? And the damp sand of your thighs, and the musk of the root just dug, and moonlight ripening Persephone's jeweled fruit, each wet red seed a blooddrop with a tooth inside. And I may come to love yet your old-woman smells of warm wax, of wet wood, of vinegar and the pinched wick, the way I already love the struck match, the blown wick, and larvae rotting in the smoked-out hive.

How could a man not love the night even in her self-absorption, even her neediness? How could I not love you whom Hecate loves in all your weathers, hot cold wet or dry? How could I not love the winds tame or wild that, at six, at seven, I took to be the body of the god; and knew then our weather was God's moods, storm and calm of one flesh with the thoughts inside his mind? How could I not love the wind, God's breath on earth, and the sea, we know who she is, the sea; and her sister the earth; and the rain, rain too, rain tame or wild? And I think the night must love me very much, since sometimes in the night I have felt your love like rain, like the thinnest mist, falling softly on my face and arms.

IV

JONATHAN LAZARUS WRIGHT

1702-1729

from fever after falling in a well

I saw trees walking upside down across
Small Hill, the stone spires reared to toss
black gravel by the handful down the well
and make the water bubble. My hands swell
like breaddough under linen on a sideboard
where shadows whisper, the banked firecoals hiss
and squint into the smoke for Lazarus
who passed his sister, stitching, when he fell.
"Four days he's lain there, Lazarus will smell. . . ."
I smell her throat raw from crying. Lord,
don't let them hold my head up to the damp
beards of elders while the rainclouds tap
white canes against the door to be let in
and someone curses, fumbling with a lamp.
Let the barber take a razor to my chin.

The housedogs, wakened from their evening nap,
growl just the way that sets each other off
like yawning during Sermon, the first cough
which Father likened to Original Sin.
Faces dissolve like bread on water when
we fished for horned pout with a common pin,
the millwheel creaking, the tailrace foaming brown
as bock beer sloshed from hogsheads that time the Crown
and Anchor's publican was whipped through town.
Hope noses my hand open, her puppies sniff,
snort, claw the pineboards, whine, slink back to lick
the poison oozing from my blistered feet
like lambfat dripping onto blackened brick.
A great bird flaps above me, a white sheet
is lowered to lift me skyward in a sling.
Christ butterflies a bent nail to a string.

Doña Sebastiana

A battered pail of ash
with a baling wire handle
beside the altar, lit
by a flailing candle.
The Lenten rituals.
The upstroke that wets
the living skin of the walls,
dripping with regrets.

While some kiss Christ's cold feet
and bear the crucifix
until one shoulder burns,
and a thin man kneels
his way over broken bricks,
and a young man, cutting deals,
bets a month of rosaries
that San Caetano
won't lift his crown of thorns
until the Virgin heals,
Doña Sebastiana,

La Muerte, in her cart,
comes creaking on wooden wheels.

Once, her lips could pout!
Today, she has no lips,
no stomach for love-play,
no garden whose bouquet
turned men's heads her way,
their pockets inside out.

Her hourglass breasts and hips,
blasted by time's sands,
slipped quickly through the hands
she's holding out to you,
once soft and so petite.
No meat's left on the bone.

Her wintry passion's spent—
more glancing light than heat—
like a fire in straw,
soon kindled, soon put out
beneath her stamping feet
that kicked against the law.

Her scraped bones, pared
of the flesh they bore
show she has no heart.
And yet all men ignore
the warning these bones give—
each one wants to live
forever in Paradise,
although all lack that art
since Eve and Adam's start,

and so must come to this,
her clutch, her lipless kiss
that sticks to our lips like ice.

We're immortal till we're thirty,
then we kneel to pay Death court.
As soon as her back is turned,
"Damn that whore!" we cry.
"She goes with everyone!"

But at the little death
love suffers us to taste,
our limbs so interlaced
we drink each other's breath,
our blood cries "Viva La Muerte!"

The white shock of her head
crackles in the air.
Her arms are open wide.
They keep the shape the bow
has drawn her limbs into.
A cinder whistles through
her ribs, washed with lime.
We bow and catch the scent
of burnt hair and sour wine.

Her braced legs are set square,
though skinny, like a bird
of prey's upon its perch.
That arch, through which we passed
to force our entry here,
will swallow us at last.
Her hollow sockets search
our faces for a sign.

Back Home

for Melissa Green

Last time I visited, I saw despair's
scabbed hash-marks healing
on your slender wrist. I heard life's thin voice
calling from downstairs.
The old ones made their grievings their careers,
set to verses by the lips I never kissed
in greeting. Your mother gone,
your father dead, daily
your hands still smooth the wrinkles from their bed.
And still his words beat hotly in your ears,
her blood calls down the moon that lays you low
as in your childhood, when he used to row,
after he'd lost her,
in winter, at night, drunk,
the ocean to Egg Rock.

Small body prone
to the world's whitecapped welt,
you hugged your ribs and felt
the attic floorboards roll beneath your weight,
waves breaking onto shingle, the same slate
as the parched chalkboard where you read your fate
and tried to sponge it out.

Downstairs, the handbell's rung.

Barefoot at midnight in the empty street,
a nightgown wrapping you in its white mist,
up to your ankles in the freezing sleet,
another worksheet crumpled in your fist,
you face the wind
and let the salt from Gloucester bite your tongue.

Less terrible than when the branch you swung
from let you down
by the neck to the ground
when you were eight, and life was hell.

Again, the bell has rung.
In bed, your father's mother,
one of life's short-timers, bids you come.
Begs you, begs you, begs you, re-enlist.

Downstairs, the wind blows through the rooms,
and it is years.

Your poems are candles lit
in the ocean-facing windows of your house
to such keen absences.

By their light, I watch you pour
a glass of water for
your *lares* and *penates*—
their worshipper and would-be exorcist.

Again, the bell.

Let the dead die.

Friend,
I wish you well.

Gaea

Broad-hipped, this earth-mother twists to check
the marbled stretchmarks, fingering her waist;
hard muscular contractions, the torque of her neck
drove a sculptor mad but kept him chaste.

Commissioned work. A betting against the clock.
His hands shake as he sets the day's first drink,
files, points, and chisels on the shaping block
whose virgin coolness still hurts his head to think.

It heals so slowly! A month, and then a month . . .
the hairline fracture where her ankle took
the stress of stepping to her scabbled plinth
from the leafed pages of his graphpaper sketchbook.

Was it luck or the pressure of deadlines left unlaced
that sandal slipping from the favored heel,
pink from her bath, a towel's chance folds placed
like shock-waves spreading from the cleft his chock
tapped open where it waited in the rock
to be engendered by a slip of steel?

The Fire

I woke and found a fire in my desk
that burned for weeks. I couldn't put it out.
Its brightness cast my former days in doubt.
It seemed I'd sleepwalked through a perpetual dusk.

The fire lapped ink as if it were lamp oil.
Devouring letters from a few old flames,
it whispered, trying to memorize their names,
then whistled like a kettle on the boil

as its eyes undressed the women there
(some snapshots from a packet on a shelf)
one like a lion in her tawny hair,
and rendered Eve a shadow of herself.

Its flames were the lateen sails of Egyptian ships
plying Cleopatra down the Nile.
They snapped like branches when the ripe figs of her lips
parted for the empire's rank and file.

Soot tacked up its bunting of black crepe
in scalloped swatches from drawer to pigeonhole.
My notebook bowed its spine and bared its nape.
My inkwell was smoking like a lit pipe bowl.

Skywriting lined my ceiling's bare white boards!
What I glimpsed through panes of shifting haze
was dozens of upside-down capital *A*'s
that hung like crutches on the walls at Lourdes.

Blue smoke filled up my lungs and cramped my chest.
A fledgling lay moulting in my veins. Sour ash
was what it fed on. Its beak was a red gash.
Each night it settled on a different nest:

my German grammar from North Junior High;
three squat, unstoppered inkpots that hissed and dripped
their river of forgetfulness; the snipped
blond locks of landlocked Waltham's Lorelei.

Five ledgers reddened by its brooding there
burst into flames. I brought it offerings—
a plate of pencils that one wing swept bare.
I listened stiffly as it whispered things

I had told no one. How could it have known
the night I held my arm into the flame
and how my heart grew heavy as a stone
and how many times since then, the same, the same?

I sat impassive as it polished off
the knobs and Gothic tracery atop
the cabinet that held my manuscript.
Its sharp beak bit down on the nib I gripped.

Fire trembled above my pen like a lit wick.
Then night shook out her braid of scorched black hair.
My meditations sent the yellowing smoke
of what I loved of earth into the air.

Like vultures in a kettle, charred scraps rode
their widening spiral higher. Wings pressed flat,
one clung to a rafter like a fat black bat
over my notebook, into which there snowed

a guano of white-out. Each ruled leaf
ceded with an ease the difficult
words my blunt pen had ploughed. The page went deaf
one letter at a time. But still the milt

of oblivion thickened, big globs dropped
tears of spilled milk for the phrase they would erase,
my eyes were whited like Tobias's,
my notebook rose like dough. The cheap stock sopped.

Then dissolution or a kind of grace
descended the metal chakras of its spine.
The fire's white flags were flapping in my face
as it surrendered to a silence wholly mine.

Moon,

I think you would understand
my craft of writing, how it makes of me
your king and creature in this no-man's-land
of the moment;
the wide-eye, squint-eye vision that by turns
I loose upon your beauty, my soft palm
and callused fingers of an archer's hand;
and how my introspection bends me to
you, filling the mirror of this blank white sheet
with your circle of renewed virginity
that, by violating, I complete.

Bella Roma

Junked hypodermics made it hard to walk
along the Tiber by the deserted, grand
sandstone embankment of the temple block.
In the river, itself the color of umber mud under sand,
two navy frogmen hugged us for a block.
The bubbles from their air tanks pocked
the water. Twin snorkels rose to slice
the sleazy surface. An inflated lifeboat
weighed down by officers in summer whites
was making progressively tighter figure 8's,
drawing in nets with water bottle floats.
A cardinal streaked by in a chauffeured launch,
pudgy fingers folded flat against his paunch.
His backwash brought the frogmen to a boil.
A fisherman smashed his rod. He wolfed the bait,
cold anchovies in a film of oil
on bread rounds from a blinding china plate.
Glass masks flashed in the sun. Underfoot,

the needles crunched, a dusting of Alpine ice
or wedding rice.
By the Ripetta, my paesano, a New Englander,
lived in a certain stone locanda, for there
a drying pair
of some Celtics fan's green-topped socks
finished the flag on a red window box.
Augustus still smiles on his slaves and their latest gods.
In that poor soil, a bursting milkweedpod's
silk purse was turning to a sow's cracked ear.
I thought of Circe. My Sicilian muse
burned to no purpose in the dog days' heat
and the dust of the street.
The sulphurous Tiber sputtered like a fuse.
The noon hour made the city's scizzy air
taste like *soldi,* like holy water from the scalloped fonts
of Santa Maria del Populo. Navona Square
was huge and carless, but some days a sick fog haunts
its waters, and our hired guide said it stains
everything except the orphaned kids
who get the pennies if they clean the drains.
I came by bus each evening to watch the rain's
glass ampules shatter on Neptune's heavy lids.
A black river issues from the catacombs
of the Metro exit
to swamp St. Peter's Square and kiss his foot—
a filthy custom, some contend, but, *ut
poetice loquar,*
not every pilgrim can kiss Pope John Paul's ring.
Each day's sky is a vast rotunda, its glass dome

consumes the music of our suffering.
In Rome, all roads lead away from Rome.
The altar's roped off like a boxing ring.

Nocturne

for James and Pamela Morton

Over St. John's spire
the cross hangs fire.

So, like a switchblade
quivering in its mark,
pinning down the boundary
of Harlem after dark,

a crane's steel spire
slices open the air.
Reflected in a pothole's
black basin, it vibrates there.

Around it, the sirens
and electronic car alarms
broadcast their flashes.
A woman with folded arms

and Four Roses on her breath
walks these blocks barefoot.
A coat on a crutch sells meth.
On the Cathedral roof,

standing under the lights
for safety, the Archangel Gabriel
lifts his horn of plenty
over Morningside Heights.

Above the martyrs and saints
now lost in the general dark,
he trumpets the Resurrection
over Morningside Park.

Across the street, laughter
brightens the night in gusts
swirled from a door. The cafe's
steel skirt is flecked with rust.

Outside the Hungarian,
on the coats of parishioners
crossing the walkway, myrrh's
scent of redemption mixes

with coffee and paprika—
on earth as it is in heaven?
The cooks are from Budapest,
the dishwashers, Dominica.

(But in La Rosita's, the scent
of candles lit for Mary's
intercession mixes
with arroz con calamares.)

Under a striped awning
on a sagging cardboard box
Angel deals three-card monte
and his brother sells socks.

A high-strung violin,
its bow sawing raw nerves,
murders its phrase again.
Wet headlights swerve

on the slick street to avoid
a ghostly somnambulist.
The driver's "Fuck you!" echoes
off cars through the fiberglass mist.

A quick red fox
in spikes and a mini goes by.
The blind beggar on his corner
hawks, and spits at the sky.

One eye on the action,
one eye on the block,
Angel flips the club queen
over on her back.

And the rain comes down in spades.
Black notes torn from the score
of the storm make Little Cuba's
dirt lot an Everglades.

Tires squeal. A woman screams.
Sweet jangle of shattering glass.
Or is it the wind-chimes
outside Moon Palace?

A posse of teenage girls,
cornrows, pigtails, and braids,
prick their victims with pins
they say are infected with AIDS.

A mother and her daughter
bum coins. The girl shivers hard,
watching loaves steam in a window.
A clock glares down like a guard.

The gypsy naps between palms.
A cop wrestles with a pencil
stub. The traffic jam's
horns blow as each driver

slows for a good look.
A man sells one fork on a cloth.
The cop writes. The rain
blurs the words in his book.

In the neon windows of bars
glacial raindrops trace
a lifetime's wrinkles and scars
on an undergraduate face.

There's a queue for umbrellas. Not bread,
but the rain's disposable needles
are what we share with the poor.
Sirens stain everything red.

Taillights. The violin.
Pain, and pain's one note
held like a blade
to the night's throat.

December 27, 1988

Another rape in the trains, a drunk torched in the park.
Last night I heard their voices through the dark
screen of dreams a pill drew round my head,
circling and circling. Last night I dreamt my city's dead
alive and dying in our double bed.

                                        It was late
for fishing, but a black man with a jackknife sliced
his liver for bait and laid it on the rail,
then set the knife down on a paper plate,
patting his pockets for a cloth to wipe
away the grease.
A Doberman dragged a white man on a leash
toward the orangey meat.
The owner swore and whipped his pet mid-leap
with the leash, but the black man's bent back caught
the leather, turning, which he did to keep
the dog from wrapping its tongue around the blade.
I watched the putty-colored grit

of gizzards thicken on a brick he'd laid
for weight atop his cooler's squeaking lid.
A woman, a girl really, just a kid,
was climbing through a squeaking subway grate
naked, but wrapped in a jacket.
I thought it hurt the girl to watch her, but
she was so opened. I saw her rusty cuts,
the blue bruise and the gooseflesh on her thigh,
the clots of cinders dripping from her hair.
She turned. A fist had made a mess of her left eye.
Still, she stared straight
through me. "Speak," she said.
I studied the slick stain fading from the rail.
The scattered strips of liver never hit
the water, for a sudden flock
of birds descended from the empty air.
A seagull with a singed beak nailed
its dole mid-air. Then the smell of rice
and diesel on the wind refreshed the pier.
When the wind dropped, she began to speak.

"My tongue was frozen to the rail's blue ice.
I couldn't scream or cry. I heard the click of dice
shaken and shaken from a plastic cup
each time the wheels slowed, stopped, and started up—
a local. He slapped me every time I shut my eyes.
I heard my fortune being whispered in the hiss
of winds through papers when the express passed,
shaking down streetlight through a metal grate
over where he took me. The papers lay still.
The rats came scratching. The reek of piss
was eating through my hair into my head.

I felt the thunder coming down the rails.
It's fear that does you. It is not the pain,
except when he cut me with the half-inch nails
untrimmed on his thumbs.
When the blood began to well, I turned my head.
When he was finished, he watched me for a while.
He smashed some bricks and spat to wet the red
paste, and scribbled with it
on the ties and rails and all around my head.
I woke to cold rain
on my cheek, the same taste of the galvanized
light through the grate. I opened my eyes. My eye.
Bootsoles scraped across my square of sky.
I was alone. But I was miles
from any place where tokens turned the stiles
and men and women talked, and help could come.
I woke to a bricked-in heart
scratched by its arrow, a rusty nail,
in the tar on a tie.
I woke to this body and a stick of gum
balanced next to my number etched on the rail,
and sometimes in the dark I see his eyes."
Then I knelt and took the girl's dead weight
under the armpits, to lift her through the grate.
Her body heaved.
She might have been crying, but she made no sound.

"We are living ballast for the ship of state
that's dumped us here, now it's gone aground."
I looked to see who said this. As I turned around,
a madman with a ferret passed me by,
swinging a hatchet as he clicked the locks

on the shopping cart he'd made into a cage,
linked to his belt-loop by a chain of socks.
His snow-white hair was turning blue with age.
His nicotine-stained fingers raked his beard
"to meet Ophelia when the moon appeared."
The ferret worked its treadmill in a rage,
making the whole cart shake.
The man stooped to light up, and as he stood he blew
the smoke out in a plume, then smiled and drew
a green stem deftly through a buttonhole,
a leaf of ivy "for her pretty sake."
Then he stood straight and catechized his soul,
reading the questions from a paperback
he'd scotchtaped to an armstrap of his pack,
answering each question with the same wet cough.
He gave himself a grade of "*F* for fair,"
lungs wheezing like a pitchpipe while he tried
to find the hatchet slapping against his side,
now hanging from his neck on a leather thong.
He adjusted his butane lighter to a flare,
then gravely shook his head and started off,
making up phrases for the marching song
his hatchet whistled to the chilly air,
wind ruffling the long blue plumage of his hair.
A man with his shirt on fire
stepped from the grass onto the path. His left hand tore
at yesterday's headlines packed against his skin,
a sheaf of flames
under the tattered jacket that he wore,
now a coat of ash,
a carbon copy of his former coat.
His right hand pressed

an empty to bare hipbone when his vest
went up in smoke. His eyewhites set like hard
boiled eggs in their sockets, and I smelled the tarred
crossties from the subway's switching yard,
but his face was afloat
and lay rocking on his neck like an open boat
above the rustling foam of the incoming tide.
He was awash,
picking his feet high as if he walked uphill.
When the wave that he was riding uncapped to crash
and glass splinters glittered
round him on his downward, tarred
path, the *Thunderbird* label wasn't even charred.
His foot was feeling for less shaky ground.
Then I saw a drop
of red wine wobble on his bottom lip.
His black tongue raced the flames to lick it dry.
Only then did he open his mouth and start to cry,
screaming for Jesus as the flames climbed higher
till each hair on his head was a red-hot wire.
I woke then when I felt how the subway slid
toward Harlem beneath my feet but I heard no sound.

Now I walk this boat basin path, awake.
A tugboat drags dull colors through the wake
rejoining behind it.
Dirt thickens the river. This souther's
kicking up a chop, and the smell of rice
from the houseboats rises, warm and comforting.

Foam fenders chafe on a pier, and there's the ring
of a shackle against a mast in the lifting wind,
the reek of tar when a tinner's scissors glint from a roof.

A thaw has rotted the ice.
Last night's voices come in gusts and are blown away.
Now others like me have arrived to watch the end
of sunlight on another busy day.
Still, I cannot shake
what I heard them say.

I see the Massacre of the Innocents
in brick dust on old snow, the red
haze sifting through a chain link fence.
I see the girl's face in the station's glow.

"Speak," she insisted. A wind rose in me. I spoke.
Now green things seek me out. A living tongue
is what I'd give them, but my heart's the wrung-
out towel my mother gave her son to suck.

Tomorrow's predicted wet east wind will smear
St. Mary's churchbells on her raw walls and tear
an opening in the coat of this sharkskinned year.
Sun, I want to follow where you lead me, but
your last rays weld the Hudson's bronze doors shut.

V

The Black Bull

The black bull fills the ditch's width.
His swayback spine curves like a snathe's thrawn grain,
the dips and rises of the Inveragh Road,
tarred crown and shoulders glistening in rain.

His tail is the bell-pull for the porter of hell-gate.
Here, where everything's stunted, stripped trees
tilt the hillside. His head is bladed with hate.
A third horn shrinks back, wet, between his knees.

His horns are forked lightning. Each smithed shiv
is twinned, so his mind is split
like the snaketongue Patrick lashed to the pulpit.
The white wake on the bay is its negative.

Elsewhere, invaders come astride a horse.
Not this hedged island. Here, the Golden Horde's
a troop afoot, means whins, the thorny gorse
that spreads like yellow fever through the wards.

His nearest neighbors are these: wingbeat
of hawk; uneaten feet and scream of its kill;
thorn; murderous thistle; the bloodwort caught
red-handed with its fingers in the till.

Cows graze on fog that's rising in the leas.
The black bull bellows to the sea's
roar, mounting. His nostrils breathe forth brine.
Next spring, the milk will smack of iodine.

By fields too small to fit both plough and horse,
his tufty stomach is a black sun hung
over the roadstones. Two brothers, farmers, curse
each other and fight with pitchforks over his dung

though there is dung enough to go around.
Lime boulders like snow cleared to the side of the road
drip in the sun. But the blown
sea foam lies white and will not melt. Is stone.

His withers are dimpled where a fist or the tip
of a sword once rested. Tons of impending light
that buffed and brushed his hide from horn to hip
slice through his skull and make the morning bright.

His head is a beaked anvil held by the wind.
His nose shines in the sun
like the priest's new patent leather shoes.
You'll find his like in each parish and precinct.

Wind-licked, his eye is a clean black slate. Watch him.
Wherever a fingerpad is rolled and inked
under pressure of a sergeant's thumb,
his pupils are the pigment that they use.

Black night is lodged there. Deep inside his head,
on thick jet velvets and soot silks of char,
one cinder glimmers. Pasiphae is spread
over his horn, conceiving the Minotaur.

His head is heavy with the dark earth smells
of flint and peat. His each eye-slit,
a crescent ember, midnight's moonlet.
In his hoofprint, the whole Atlantic wells.

Rain. Wind. Salt bite of waves in the bay
crumbling a cliff and the high sea's sound
are nothing to him. A day and a night and a day
break on his back. He sleeps, holding his ground.

Treblinka

Still, when the wind is right,
lying awake in bed,
I hear the all-night shunting of the cars.

Once, in a lull,
the sound of a fountain
or the distant tinkling of bells.
And there stepped into my head
a girl with coins
sewn into her hem,
holding her little sister by the hand.

I had met her before,
the friend of a friend,
in a crowd at the midsummer fair.
Like me, she was nine or ten.

They were with us,
lost in the funhouse,

until the fat
lady sat and spread
their cards on her lap.
I laughed till my face turned red
when the hypnotist made the mayor
bark like a dog as he read
the fate allotted them there.
My yarmulke hurt my head,
so I took it off.

Then the fat lady's husband, the thin
man who only ate pins
(not counting angels), drew
from the depths of his feathered hat
numbers he stitched in green
ink to their skin.

Sleek as a crow in the wood
in his blue-black top hat and tails,
the monocled ringmaster stood.
The coins in his hand rang like bells.

As the girls were taken away,
the clown hid me under his coat.
I heard the gypsy say:

"O Poland, you slept
while the blue tongues of flames
christened your children,
but the leaves remember our names

who fell like leaves
in the city of bells."

Then the sun went into eclipse
and smoke grew thick as the crows
over Kraków, Warsaw, and Belzec.

Last night,
clear through the cold air,
over the guttural purring of cars,
I heard small bells again.
How thin
she had grown where she lay
alone on the grain
of gravel!

All the bells were gone.
All I heard was wind.
The bare branches of trees
creaked like the knobs of her knees
as she stood.
The wind in some clumps of grass
hissed like escaping gas
at her feet. Her hip
shifted under the heft
of a stone she had to lift.
I heard it grate as she wrote
God, do not let my sister die
on a concrete wall
from right to left.

I saw her sister try
on a shoe from a pile of shoes.
Just then, out of the blue,
a loudspeaker crackled and called
a number I knew.

I liked striking tents the best,
and the act with the big cats and chairs,
and days between shows on the road.
Leopards are hardest to tame.

My new family was good
to me, and besides,
where else would I go?
We went to church a day late;
otherwise, life was the same.

Switzerland was nice.
I danced with a bear on the ice
of the Rhein—or was it the Rhône?
And there was a trick with a knife
I kept trying to hone.

Later, some of us let
the black-robed magistrates
Americanize our names
when we got to the States.

You can never be sure
who was who in the war.
You can't always trust what you hear.

Holy Mother, how
could you be the Heilige Jungfrau
of Belsen and Birkenau?

White Nights, 1938

Russia, your white nights,
a blizzard of linen for lovers once,
have come to mean witch-hunts,
a litter of letters and lives
thrust under the lights
of a surgical theater, and knives
scraping a phrase from the skin
of a sheep or a goat.
Since you've used them for vellum,
the ranks of your poets grow thin.

My Love Has Been

the full moon
on fresh snow, a red fox vixen
and the pack following.

Lunes

Today is a black feather and a six
at each toss of the die.

The dawn sun, a scab
on the horizon.

Today the dogs
got what they wanted.

Today is sixty stitches,
puffy faces bobbing by.

Sunset:
impetigo and iodine.

Tomorrow is the dull thud of a hammer
and a knotholed sky.

Tomorrow is today
for someone unluckier than I.

Last night poured
gasoline on my childhood!

Today is all ellipsis: a red ant clinging
to the escarpment of a lip.

No, César. It's only Monday. *Lunes.* Monday.
Don't die. Not here. Not yet.

¿Dónde, Federico?
¿Dónde?

This morning is downpour
and runoff.

A black feather and a six
at each toss of the die!

El Niño

This month,
even the rain,
the stone god Tlaloc,
an anvil cloud his hat,
squats, backed to a rock,
huddles like us,
gnawing his knees.

Landing in Cairo

for Carol Moldaw

Dawn.

A white sail
on the horizon, a blade
in the sun, a flame.

Wind in the palms.

The crackling of tactical maps
to Octavius,
bringing back
this dream:

his face
dipped in gold,
crossing the gypsy's palm.

Antony
stirs.

Wind flickering
the flaps
of the white tent, lit
like a lantern
from within.

Cleopatra!

The chalky columns
and alabaster busts
of Rome can't hold a candle
to this
basilisk,
her eyelids heavy with an eternal dusk.

"And did you lie abed when Caesar—"

"Don't speak
to me of Caesar.
The bees
have eaten him."

Now Antony will gladly trade the sand
of the Circus Maximus for this arena,
the red oval of her love-bite on his hand.

All the past
devoured
in love's holocaust.

The fish will come
already salted onto his hook

until Actium:

white wings beating—
the sails of her ships,
bees
streaming from the hive.

Landing in Cairo, my jet's
exhaust smudging the desert,
I thought of you in Rome.

Below us,
lapis and sapphire jeweled
the ramparts.

As we taxied toward the terminal,
the silver
sliver of moon
topping a mosque
pricked my heart.

I, too, was coming back
from weeks of thirst and fast,
my lips blistered from the sun,
returning to you.

Blue and purple-blue
blossoms dotted the airstrip's
infield. Like blossoming water,
the lily of the Nile.

My lily of the Nile,
I was the tongue
licking your lips,

I was the bee buzzing among
the agapanthus' bristling minarets.

Sunstruck, dizzy,
I lay dozing in the sun.

Two guards with Uzis patrolled
the open doors of the plane
while we refueled.

We nosed into the wind
on the runway
behind airships
bound for Jiddah, Tunis, Dubai,
Tamanrasset, Dar es Salaam,
Adis Abeba, Djibouti, Khartoum.

Fragrant names!
I asked for a blessing beyond men.

Dawn.

A first poppy opens.
All the past
happens.

And still the day is young.

The dawn wind.

Desire.

A white sail,
a blade catching the sun.

For us, too, love, these sheets
hold the rustle of flames.

O, Sheba!
O, Solomon!

Note

These books provided details and background material on the Penitentes for "The High Road to Taos" and "Doña Sebastiana":

Echoes of the Flute by Lorenzo de Cordova

Santos and Saints by Thomas J. Steele, S.J.

Brothers of Light Brothers of Blood by Marta Weigle.

Illinois Poetry Series

Laurence Lieberman, Editor

History Is Your Own Heartbeat
Michael S. Harper (1971)

The Foreclosure
Richard Emil Braun (1972)

The Scrawny Sonnets and
Other Narratives
Robert Bagg (1973)

The Creation Frame
Phyllis Thompson (1973)

To All Appearances: Poems New
and Selected
Josephine Miles (1974)

The Black Hawk Songs
Michael Borich (1975)

Nightmare Begins Responsibility
Michael S. Harper (1975)

The Wichita Poems
Michael Van Walleghen (1975)

Images of Kin: New and
Selected Poems
Michael S. Harper (1977)

Poems of the Two Worlds
Frederick Morgan (1977)

Cumberland Station
Dave Smith (1977)

Tracking
Virginia R. Terris (1977)

Riversongs
Michael Anania (1978)

On Earth as It Is
Dan Masterson (1978)

Coming to Terms
Josephine Miles (1979)

Death Mother and Other Poems
Frederick Morgan (1979)

Goshawk, Antelope
Dave Smith (1979)

Local Men
James Whitehead (1979)

Searching the Drowned Man
Sydney Lea (1980)

With Akhmatova at the Black Gates
Stephen Berg (1981)

Dream Flights
Dave Smith (1981)

More Trouble with the Obvious
Michael Van Walleghen (1981)

The American Book of the Dead
Jim Barnes (1982)

Counting the Black Angels
Len Roberts (1994)

National Poetry Series

Eroding Witness
Nathaniel Mackey (1985)
Selected by Michael Harper

Palladium
Alice Fulton (1986)
Selected by Mark Strand

Cities in Motion
Sylvia Moss (1987)
Selected by Derek Walcott

The Hand of God and a
Few Bright Flowers
William Olsen (1988)
Selected by David Wagoner

The Great Bird of Love
Paul Zimmer (1989)
Selected by William Stafford

Stubborn
Roland Flint (1990)
Selected by Dave Smith

The Surface
Laura Mullen (1991)
Selected by C. K. Williams

The Dig
Lynn Emanuel (1992)
Selected by Gerald Stern

My Alexandria
Mark Doty (1993)
Selected by Philip Levine

The High Road to Taos
Martin Edmunds (1994)
Selected by Donald Hall

Other Poetry Volumes

Her Soul beneath the Bone:
Women's Poetry on Breast Cancer
Edited by Leatrice Lifshitz (1988)

Days from a Dream Almanac
Dennis Tedlock (1990)

Working Classics:
Poems on Industrial Life
*Edited by Peter Oresick and
Nicholas Coles* (1990)

Hummers, Knucklers, and
Slow Curves: Contemporary
Baseball Poems
Edited by Don Johnson (1991)

The Double Reckoning of
Christopher Columbus
Barbara Helfgott Hyett (1992)

Selected Poems
Jean Garrigue (1992)

New and Selected Poems, 1962-92
Laurence Lieberman (1993)

811.54   Edmunds, Martin,
EDM   1955-

          The high road to
          Taos.

BAKER & TAYLOR